So you really want to

English

Book Three
Answer book

So you really want to learn

English

Book Three
Answer book

Susan Elkin

Series Editor: Nicholas Oulton M.A. (Oxon.)

GALORE PARK

www.galorepark.co.uk

Published by Galore Park Publishing Ltd
19/21 Sayers Lane, Tenterden, Kent TN30 6BW

www.galorepark.co.uk

Text copyright © Susan Elkin 2006

The right of Susan Elkin to be identified as the author of this Work has
been asserted by her in accordance with sections 77 and 78 of the
Copyright, Designs and Patents Act 1988.

Typography by Typetechnique, London W1

Printed and bound by CPI Antony Rowe, Chippenham

ISBN-13: 978 1 902984 93 3

First published 2006, reprinted 2007, 2009

Details of other Galore Park publications are available at
www.galorepark.co.uk

ISEB Revision Guides, publications and examination papers may also
be obtained from Galore Park.

Contents

Introduction

So you really want to learn English Book 3 is intended for pupils in Year 8 and for scholarship candidates. It takes users through everything that they will need for Common Entrance and scholarship examinations and offers plenty of opportunity for extension into off-piste learning and development – especially through wider reading. Most of the proposed themes for Common Entrance are visited and threaded through the chapters.

Some of the chosen extracts are deliberately very challenging. Every teacher will have his or her own way of helping pupils to meet that challenge at an appropriate level and there are plenty of my thoughts and responses in this Answer Book. And, perhaps every teacher would do well do put, writ large on the classroom wall, T S Eliot's famous maxim: 'Poetry can communicate before it is understood'. No English teacher should expect pupils to understand, on first acquaintance, everything there is to understand about some of the finest writing in English. They are, after all, at the very beginning of a life-long learning adventure.

Users of the pupil's book will soon be transferring to senior school – hence the introduction to topics like First World War literature and the multifarious functions of language which they will need as they head toward GCSE.

Susan Elkin
July 2006

Chapter 1

Exercise 1.1

1. Mrs Danvers must be a servant because she has made the bed and arranged the flowers. She is evidently quite senior in the household (not just a maid) since she has discussed the architecture of the house with the narrator.

2. Suggestions only: (a) wrapped, covered, shrouded (b) swarthy, yellow, unwell (c) initials, personal mark, name.

3. She is Mrs de Winter, because Rebecca was a de Winter and the narrator has married the same man.

4. The narrator is nervous and curious. She has gone exploring and opened the door because she wants to know what's there, but suffers a shock and panics momentarily ('For one desperate moment I thought that something had happened to my brain') when she sees Rebecca's things. She seems jealous of Rebecca and envies her glamorous possessions ('things I would have loved and almost worshipped had they been mine'). She wants to know more about her predecessor to such an extent that she smells and touches her nightdress in a faintly repellent way. Sometimes though she empathises with Rebecca. (For example, she understands why the other woman had used one hairbrush more than the other.)

5. Rebecca's apricot nightdress and her scents and powder suggest that she was more confident and more assertively feminine than the 'sallow and plain' narrator with her 'hair hanging lank and straight.' Rebecca's room is full of expensive possessions. So she was more flamboyant than the narrator who obviously does not have such things because she envies them and the glamour they represent. But Rebecca is 'in the crypt of the church with all the other dead de Winters'. So she is effectively a ghost in this passage. The narrator is frightened by Rebecca's presence because she can almost see, smell and hear her. Her legs tremble as she waits in vain for something to happen. Strangely, the dead Rebecca is stronger in this extract than the living narrator.

6. She is disturbed by the fact that the nightdress has not been laundered since Rebecca last wore it. She can see creases in it made by Rebecca's body and she can smell the remains of her scent. It makes Rebecca seem physically present.

Exercise 1.2

1. They are highly mysterious because they seem to have been made and installed thousands of years ago by ancient people who, obviously, had no modern lifting gear. People puzzle about why there are so many and wonder what their purpose can have been. There is unlikely ever to be a definite answer.

2. Suggestions only: (a) currents, waves, storms (b) system of lifting weights by raising them up with long rods or levers (c) invaded and took over government.

3. Sweet potatoes were their staple food but these vegetables are not indigenous to Easter Island. Scientists do not know how they arrived on Easter Island from the Americas, the nearest part of which is over 2000 miles away.

4. The theory is that the long-eared people of Easter Island were the elite who ruled over the short-eared workers. It was the aristocracy who were commemorated in the statues.

5. Thor Heyerdahl knew that no one would believe that the Pacific Ocean could be crossed in the sort of small flimsy craft that the Polynesians would have had. So he built a replica raft and made the journey to show that it could be done.

6. The statues serve no practical purpose. Like medieval cathedrals in Europe, they would have required an enormous, collaborative labour effort to carve, transport and place in position. On the whole it is only religion which motivates human beings to such extreme endeavours.

7. It is thought that ropes were wrapped round the statue with a long length hanging from each side. The statue itself then functions as a pulley. One group of men hauls on one side. They are counterbalanced by a similar group on the other rope. If they haul alternately it would be possible to ease the statue a very short distance forward.

8. It is difficult to be sure of the age of the DNA which has been examined. Ancient Polynesians would not have left their DNA because their bodies were cremated after death.

Exercise 1.3

1. The first three stanzas are narrated by some sort of storyteller who questions the ailing knight-at-arms. From the fourth stanza we hear the knight's own account of what has happened to him. The poem is effectively a long question, followed by a detailed answer.

2. He has been entranced by a mysterious fairy woman – 'full beautiful.' He carried her on his horse to her 'elfin grot' where they made love and she wept. He fell asleep but when he awoke he was alone in the cold outside. He is now under a spell or curse because he is 'in thrall' and can never find peace, happiness or warmth.

3. He is desolate. His face is drawn and unhappy ('haggard and woe-begone'). He cannot settle or come to terms with his loss. So with his shocked white face he just hovers ('palely loitering').

4. The birds have stopped singing. The grass on the lake has shrivelled and died. It is winter ('The squirrel's granary is full,/And the harvest's done') and it is cold on the hill's side.

5. Suggestions only: (a) afflicts, makes you ill, is upsetting you (b) horse, mount (c) bondage, slavery (d) wait, pass my days, linger.

6. This is open ended. The possibilities include:

    'horrid': this word has a changed meaning; it had a much stronger meaning. Originally it was associated with horror.

    'sighed full sore': the alliterative sibilants ('s' and 'f') make it mysterious.

    'roots of relish sweet': there is an implication that she drugged him.

Exercise 1.5

1. Although he was frightened, because he did not understand what was happening, James opened the door firmly but quietly.

2.   Did you really shout to frighten off any possible intruder as you entered the house, switched on the lights and noticed that something seemed to be wrong?

3.   Sit up, shut up, listen and take plenty of notes!

4.   In his novel *Bleak House*, Charles Dickens creates a character, Mr Krook, who dies through spontaneous combustion, an unexplained phenomenon which has long fascinated human beings.

5.   All over the world there are statues in Catholic churches and cathedrals, usually of the Virgin Mary, which people say they have seen weeping real, physical tears, sometimes of blood.

6.   Daphne du Maurier's best known novel dates from 1938 and, although she wrote many others, as well as some short stories and biographies, nothing ever touched the popularity of *Rebecca* except, possibly, *My Cousin Rachel* which was published in 1951.

Exercise 1.6

1.   antitheft
2.   antepenult
3.   antediluvian
4.   anticipate
5.   antenatal
6.   anticyclone

Exercise 1.7

1.   reliquaries
2.   decoys
3.   plutocracies
4.   refectories
5.   tercentenaries
6.   forays

Sample sentences:

There are several reliquaries containing relics of various saints in Siena, one of which claims to be St Peter's finger.

Because he wanted to deflect attack, the general left a few soldiers at base as a decoy to attract enemy fire away from the main body of men.

Since it is so easy to seize power if you have money, there are many countries around the world ruled by plutocracies.

Dinner was served in the refectory at 7pm each evening during our stay in the college.

2006 is the tercentenary of the birth of Benjamin Franklin in 1706.

My grandmother has made various forays into language learning and at present is working hard at acquiring Polish.

Chapter 2

Exercise 2.1

1. The main speaker is the owner of the business who is trying, by any possible means, to sell vehicles. He speaks in two different styles because sometimes she's speaking to staff such as Joe and training them in ruthless selling ('Watch the woman's face', 'Tell 'em it's just sold'). At other times he is speaking to customers politely ('Yes, sir '22 Dodge') or rudely ('Now look here mister, I ain't got all day').

2. There are coloured flags and many advertisements leading to the entrance and customers are attracted by a bargain car on a raised platform. Inside, the yard is full of vehicles and vehicle components such as tyres, exhausts, batteries and brake rods. It's noisy and smells of grease and petrol (gasoline). Sales staff watch the customers closely. The selling methods are very aggressive and once inside the office customers are made to sign contracts quickly. It's very daunting for people who have never bought a vehicle before. It is as if they are victims.

3. He knows that the customers are very unused to buying expensive items because on their farms they are more accustomed to working in the traditional ways with animals such as mules rather than with vehicles. Steinbeck shows us how nervous they are ('How do you buy a car?' 'Don't lean on that car.' 'Watch the children now'). The seller cheats them by taking items out of vehicles after they're sold and by making vehicles which don't go, appear to be working for just long enough to sell them ('squirt in a couple of quarts of sawdust').

4. Suggestions only: (a) extract, take (b) rubbish, nonsense (c) useless item (d) pushes, persuades, cons (e) dollars (between 4 and 5 US dollars to £1 in the 1930s – but remember that a pound was worth at least 20 times what it is now) (f) gypsy, traveller, beggar, lazy person (an insult).

5. The 'free' punctuation makes the passage flow very quickly. The salespeople are fast and smooth talking. The customers don't understand what's going on. They can hardly tell who is speaking or what is meant and the way the passage is punctuated reflects that. But the reader can understand how the customers are being cheated because we read/hear everything which is said. The customers hear only what the sellers want them to.

6. He has made $130. The seller paid $35 dollars for the vehicle. The customer pays $50 in cash and agrees to pay a further $40 in instalments. The seller has also taken in 'part-exchange' the customer's pair of mules and wagon which he plans to sell for $75. He has therefore taken a total of $165 of which all but $35 is profit.

Exercise 2.2

1. The fruit is 'All ripe together'. Without cold storage different fruits would normally be available in different seasons.

2. 'Come buy' is repeated as part of the sales pressure. The words also add to the rhythm of the poem because they are single syllable ones, unlike faster moving words with several syllables such as 'cranberries' and 'pomegranates'. The poet was probably used to hearing traditional London street cries – the muffin man and the cats' meat man, for example – and based these words on their calls.

3. Buyers can enjoy the fruit with their sight ('Bright-fire-like'), with touch ('bloom-down-cheeked'), with taste ('sweet to tongue').

4. The sellers, who narrate this part of the poem, are speaking fast and persuasively in order to overwhelm customers. This is the same technique that the second-hand lorry dealer uses in the *Grapes of Wrath* passage.

5. The short lines and rattling rhymes make the words tumble out very quickly. The fruits are listed and there's a lot of repetition of words ending in -berries which adds to the sense of urgency and speed. It's meant to make customers feel under pressure to buy.

Exercise 2.3

1. A 'cartel' is a group of people, companies or organisations who/which all have a similar product to sell. By working as a group they make sure that no one seller has a lower price than the others – the group agrees a price and they all charge it. It prevents undercutting, tends to cause higher prices and it works against market forces. In many countries (Britain, for example) cartels are illegal.

2. OPEC controls the world's oil prices. All countries need oil. So OPEC can affect the economies of countries which have no oil supplies of their own.

3. Two Arab states went to war with Israel in 1973. That led to OPEC, which predominately consists of Arab countries applying a trade embargo against countries such as Britain and the USA which were regarded as the enemy because of their support for Israel. Not wanting to be put in this position again, after the Arab-Israeli war, the rest of the world developed oil fields elsewhere to reduce its dependency on OPEC. That forced prices down.

4. Iraq, Iran and Nigeria have been distracted from industry by war, fears of UN sanctions and civil unrest.

5. China and India have very fast growing economies. Industry is developing rapidly in both countries so they need big oil imports to fuel their new factories and plants.

6. Demand is beginning to exceed supply. OPEC countries are pumping as much oil as they can but it isn't enough, therefore they can charge more. If oil becomes even more expensive countries will be less able to afford it, then their industries will suffer and their economies will go into recession.

Exercise 2.4

Sample sentences:

I looked up
He jumped over
She looks well
My brother tries hard
I'll go later

Exercise 2.5

Sample sentences:

Up
I ran up the hill – adverb
His business is on the up – noun
He always looks on the up side – adjective

Over
We climbed over the gate – adverb
I had mud all over me – adverb
It is all over now – adjective

Well
My mother writes very well – adverb
I went to collect water from the well – noun
She is not well – adjective

Hard
The walls were rock hard – adjective
I tried hard in all my lessons – adverb
I find maths really hard – adjective

Later
We caught a later train than usual – adjective
We danced in the later part of the evening – adjective
They arrived later than me – adverb

Exercise 2.6

Suggestions only:

1. While he was living in California John Steinbeck wrote *The Red Pony*.
2. We read 'Goblin Market' in class when we were in Year 7.
3. My mother finished the week's shopping after she had called at the school.
4. Once I have finished this exercise I shall have a rest.
5. Before they can play tennis Sam and Lucy will need their PE kit.
6. Now that oil reserves are running low the oil industry is worried.

Exercise 2.7

Sample sentences:

1. Our school crest is emblazoned on the front wall of the main building.
2. 'I seem to be beset with health problems just now,' said Granny.
3. I gazed bemused at the problem, without any idea of how to tackle it.
4. Please don't belittle my efforts because you know I am doing my best.

5.   Anne Boleyn was beheaded at the Tower of London.
6.   I don't begrudge you your prize because, although I had hoped to win it myself, I know that you really deserve it.

Exercise 2.8

1.   guava
2.   guarantor
3.   Guadeloupe
4.   guard
5.   guano
6.   guacamole
7.   guan
8.   guardian
9.   Guatemala

Chapter 3

Exercise 3.1

1. It must have been raining heavily because there is lots of mud in the streets. Horses, dogs and pedestrians are finding the roads and pavements slippery because of the water (presumably in puddles) and mud. Dense fog, worsened by the smoke from the chimneys, is making everything dark for the time of day. It is cold.

2. Suggestions only: (a) clingingly, tightly, determinedly (b) rooms in private or charitable institutions for old people – like hospital wards. Dickens could also mean small areas, like mini 'villages', in towns which are called 'wards' for the purpose of local elections (c) farmer, grower, food producer.

3. Dickens mentions the Megalosaurus and describes it as an 'elephantine lizard' to emphasise just how muddy it is underfoot – as if we were in pre-historic times and the waters were just receding to form 'dry' land. Scientists were only just discovering the dinosaurs in Dickens' time so knowledge of pre-history was a novelty. It is also an exaggeration for emphasis – known as hyperbole. And it's a joke. The idea of meeting a Megalosaurus on Holborn Hill is incongruous and comic.

4. There are no mechanical vehicles – only transport drawn by blinkered horses. There are ships with rigging and other obsolete shipping such as collier-brigs bringing coal into London. The streets and shops are lit by gas not electricity.

5. 'Compound interest' is a banking term. When you invest, say, £100 at 5% interest for a year your money is worth £105 after 12 months. That is simple interest. If you then leave your money, including the interest it has already earned, in the bank for a second year the interest will be calculated on £105. So at the end of the second year at 5% you will get £5.25 in interest because you have earned interest on your interest, as well as on the original £100 capital. That is called 'compound interest' because your interest is 'compounding' – building up – all the time.

    Dickens means that more mud sticks to the mud that is already there so it is building up like compound interest. It's an ideal metaphor for *Bleak House* which is about a long, unresolved legal case about the distribution of family money.

6. He repeats the word 'fog' thirteen times. The effect is both emphatic and humorous. You are left in no doubt that fog is the main concern of Londoners on this day. Repetition is generally avoided by writers because, used carelessly, it can be boring and lazy. Here Dickens is making a joke of deliberately pretending to be boring because fog is tiresome and tedious. More subtly, fog, which you can't see through, is a metaphor for all the misunderstandings which happen later in *Bleak House*.

Exercise 3.2

1. (a) The 'dragging grey columns' suggest rain falling thickly and heavily, straight down without the influence of sun or wind. (b) 'Glassy verticals' refers to rain so hard that it falls directly downwards and whose droplets are sharp looking and cold like pieces of glass. Both phrases, of course, indicate the relentlessness of the November rain.

2.   He sees a tramp or vagrant, asleep and impervious to the heavy rain and 'welding cold'. The man is lying in water and getting wetter but he is wearing a coat and has each hand tucked into the opposite sleeve. He has wrapped pieces of sacking round his feet for extra warmth.

3.   The student will choose but here are some possibilities, suggested as examples:

'a seep silent all summer' is interesting because the alliteration (repeated 's') and long vowel sounds ('ee' in 'seep', 'i' in 'silent' and 'a' in 'all') evoke the quiet hissing, almost menacing, sound of the rain. 'Seep' has an assonant link with 'treed' in the previous line too.

'welding cold' is effective because 'welding' suggests sticking together which is exactly what extreme cold does, for example, to fingers. It's a striking use of 'welding' also because the word is usually associated with heat and hot metal so it's really an oxymoron here. The two words are carefully chosen too for the rather chilling 'ld' sound which they share.

4.   He sees a wooden frame (gibbet) on which a gamekeeper has hung the bodies of animals he has killed because they prey on game birds. They include weasels, cats and crows, owls and hawks. It's a rather sinister sight. Some have been there a long time and are now very stiff and papery ('weightless, twirled like dry bark bits'). Others are fresher and hanging rather defiantly in the rain. Gamekeepers used to do this in the belief that other animals would see it as a warning.

5.   'Treed' means covered with trees and 'gulleyed' means threaded through with little watercourses. In both cases the coinage (or neologism) is neat and succinct. Poetry is a very concise form. Hughes is able to convey in one word what it would otherwise take several words to do – and it would be much clumsier. The long, mournful sound of both words adds to the poem's dark atmosphere too.

6.   The two poems share a title. Both are (partly) about the weather in November, the darkness and the lack of visible new life.

7.   The Hughes poem is much longer and more serious than Hood's. It reflects on the ruthless beauty of nature even in extremes of cold and wet. Hood's poem is a light-hearted lament for the lack of all the things he enjoys at other times of year. The effectiveness of Hood's poem depends on a play on words because November happens to begin with the letters 'no'.

8.   Hood has repeated the word 'no' (nineteen times) in just the same way as Dickens does with 'fog'. In both cases it's an ironic device to reinforce meaning.

Exercise 3.3

1.   The driest November weather in Britain is likely to be in East Anglia and in the eastern and central parts of the south. That means that counties like Norfolk, Surrey and Oxfordshire usually get the least rainfall in November.

2.   November can bring sudden gusts of strong winds. So gardeners should be very careful when using ladders which could be blown over. And if you spray plants in windy weather the chemicals can be blown about dangerously.

3.   Frost can kill delicate plants, so gardeners need to know when frost is expected. Then they can protect vulnerable plants.

4.   In November the coldest place in Britain is usually the east of Scotland.

5.   Unusually heavy rain caused widespread flooding in 2002.

6.   Suggestions only: (a) location, geography, the lay-out of an area (b) in a garden irrigation is artificial watering using a system which is permanently fixed so that you only have to switch it on (c) volume of fruit, vegetables or flowers which a garden yields.

Exercise 3.4

Suggestions only:

1.   some/many/enjoyable/twenty
2.   tiresome/winter/cold
3.   quickly/in a thoughtful way/during break
4.   born in the eighteenth century/a favourite of my father; fine/witty
5.   few/most/more; modern/Elizabethan/nineteenth century (and similar alternatives for the third gap)
6.   most/many/more
7.   some/cooked; tonight/tomorrow
8.   no/more/great
9.   his/my/Italian/good
10.   their/your/rock; often/sometimes/much

Exercise 3.5

1.   Thomas Hood's poems (p)
2.   dos and don'ts (o)
3.   novels written by Victorians (n)
4.   St Mary's Church (p)
5.   the reigns of Stuart Kings and Queens (n)
6.   Queen Anne's reign (p)
7.   six o'clock (o – was once 'of the clock')
8.   the witness's statement (p)
9.   we shouldn't (o)
10.   the fox's habitat (p)
11.   Guys and Dolls (n)
12.   Aunt Glynis's house (p)

Exercise 3.6

1.   I bought oranges, because they are my mother's favourite and she has a bad cold; bananas for Peter; some fresh dates, which we all like; unripe peaches, which will be ready in a few days and a big bag of overripe apples for my horse, who loves them for treats.

2.   Our tour of America took us to New England where Dad was fascinated by Boston and its history; into California where we didn't like Los Angeles but loved the countryside; eastward along the Mexican border, eventually to Louisiana and Alabama and included highlights like Charleston in South Carolina.

3.   This year Yasmin has already read three books by Charles Dickens, which she says she enjoyed very much; most of Daphne du Maurier, including *The Glass Blowers*; four modern crime novels; biographies of William Pitt and Charles Darwin and quite a lot of poetry.

Exercise 3.7

1.   farming
2.   growing grapes for wine
3.   tree cultivation
4.   beekeeping
5.   the cultivation of a single crop
6.   growing water plants and keeping water creatures

Exercise 3.8

Sample sentences:

1.   I use a pseudonym when I write book reviews for the local paper because I don't want my identity known.
2.   NATO is an acronym for North Atlantic Treaty Organisation.
3.   Many people use a cryptonym as part of their email address so that spammers cannot guess it.
4.   Hoover, Biro and Wellingtons are examples of eponyms.
5.   Once I've written 'big', 'gigantic', 'enormous', 'colossal' and 'huge', I run out of synonyms for large.
6.   My aunt announced her intention to 'leave the classroom' which she was using as a metonym for the teaching profession – so we knew that she really meant she was going to retire.

Exercise 3.9

Suggestions only – this list is not exhaustive:

arrange, array, arrears, arrest, arrive, barrel, barren, barricade, carriage, carrot, catarrh, chirrup, correction, corruption, currency, erratic, error, ferret, ferrule, ferry, garrison, horrible, horrified, hurricane, interrupt, irregular, marriage, merrily, narrate, purr, quarry, squirrel, stirrup, surrender, surround, terrace, terrible, terrific, terrified, territorial, terror, tomorrow, torrent, torrential, turret, warren, worry.

Exercise 3.10

Suggestion only:

Fog everywhere.
Fog up the river, where it flows among
Green aits and meadows;
Fog down the river, where it rolls
Defiled among the tiers of shipping,
And the waterside pollutions of a
Great (and dirty) city.
Fog on the Essex marshes,
Fog on the Kentish heights.

Chapter 4

Exercise 4.1

1. Mr Slope has red greasy hair which covers his ears lankly and is firmly brushed stickily across the top of his head. His face is very flushed and his nose looks like a red cork. He has a large mouth with thin lips, protruding brown eyes and a domed forehead. He is tall with large feet and (clammy) hands.

2. The previous bishop's name was Grantly. He is dead ('late bishop'). The clergymen (prebendaries, minor canons, clerical doctors) were 'comfortable', 'happy, well-used, well-fed'. Bishop Grantly had 'kindly wings'. So the implication is that these people have a shock coming to them.

3. Bishop Grantly's son was his chaplain. Mr Slope is now going 'to assume the station which had hitherto been filled by the son of the late bishop'. This too is clearly a big change.

4. Mr Slope means to take charge. He thinks he can become the dominant decision maker in Barchester although he's only the Bishop's assistant. He plans to be the leader, control the money in the diocese and be admired by the poor.

5. Suggestions only: (a) things, often part of the body, which stick out or protrude (b) carefully, accurately, correctly (c) roomy, spacious (d) clergymen attached to a cathedral chapter. He (or she in the 21st century) holds a prebend – a salary or piece of land. In the Church of England now 'prebendary' is sometimes an honorary title for a canon.

6. Trollope is building up an impression of a man who is very unattractive, but he is pretending to be even handed, so it's witty writing. He tells us mildly, for example, that Mr Slope's countenance (face) 'is not specially prepossessing' and then goes on to say his skin looks like bad beef and his nose like a spongy red cork. He uses the word 'intends' three times in the last paragraph to emphasise Mr Slope's ambitious determination to seize power in Barchester.

Exercise 4.2

1. The poem is narrated by the widowed Duke. He refers to his late wife as 'my last duchess'.

2. He is addressing a senior representative of a Count ('The Count your master'). He is prepared to marry the Count's daughter provided that there is a good dowry and that she and her father understand that she must obey her husband totally.

3. The Duchess has been murdered on her husband's orders ('I gave commands;/Then all smiles stopped') because he objected to the way she smiled at, and spoke to, the artist who painted her portrait and to other men in the court. The Duke is making this clear as a warning to the next possible Duchess and her family.

4. Suggestions only: 'Never to stoop', 'I gave commands', 'There she stands/As if alive.'

5. It shows that he collects very expensive art – just as he does wives. He expects them to obey him just as the sea horse is being forced to obey Neptune. It is an expression of the Duke's power. (Claus of Innsbruck is an imaginary sculptor.)

6.   Although the poem seems to flows fairly freely (in the same five beat rhythm that Shakespeare usually used) each line rhymes either with the previous or following one. This makes it seem very structured and formal. It is as if the Duke had planned very carefully in advance what he intended to say. It doesn't seem spontaneous. And that makes the warning even more menacing.

Exercise 4.3

1.   Suggestions only: (a) shifty, disreputable (b) an exceptionally talented child (c) certified by experts as genuine.

2.   The portrait is 32 inches by 25 inches, painted in oils by Johann Georg Edlinger. Although Mozart was only 34 when it was painted in 1790 it shows an ageing, unhealthy looking man. His hair is going grey. His face is puffy and his eyes have bags below them. People are surprised because familiar portraits of Mozart show a much younger man looking fit and lively.

3.   The painting was found in a neglected archive at Berlin Picture Gallery. It had been there since 1934 when the museum bought it for 650 reichsmarks. Wolfgang Seiller found it and told the curator of the gallery. Mr Seiller is an expert on Mozart. He also has remote family connections with the composer.

4.   Experts have used computers to compare the painting with an earlier painting of Mozart which hangs in an Italian gallery and is known to be genuine. The facial features match exactly, so they are completely satisfied that the subject of the newly discovered painting really is Mozart.

5.   According to Walter Hauser, the artist may have been paid after Mozart's death to make the composer look ill and as if he had lived an unhealthy or shameful life. This is possible because Mozart had extraordinary talent and many people were jealous of it. Mr Hauser is a musician, based in Salzburg and a great admirer of Mozart's music.

Exercise 4.4

1., 4., 5. and 6. need altering. 2. and 3. are correct as they stand.

Possible answers:

1.   Always tasty at Pizza Express, lunch was enjoyable.

4.   Her voice very dramatic, Fiona read her poem while the class listened.

5.   Falling on 14th February, St Valentine's Day is celebrated by lovers the world over.

6.   Inspired by Robert Browning, Andrew made it his goal to write a poem a day.

Exercise 4.5

1.   babies'
       princesses'
       ibexes'

churches'
fairies'
teachers'
headmistresses'
bushes'
scientists'
musicians'
armies'
authors'
countries'
grandmothers'
grannies'

2.   Sample sentences:

The nursery floor was strewn with babies' toys.
Princesses' rights are being renegotiated in Japan.
Ibexes' trails were very clear as we began our safari walk.
Local churches' opening times are displayed in the library.
I used to imagine fairies' houses at the bottom of my garden.
Teachers' favourite time is break!
Mrs Ibbotson is attending a headmistresses' conference this week.
Bushes' shadows fell across the country path.
I like reading about scientists' discoveries.
The Musicians' Union is a well-established body.
Various armies' vehicles were on display at the international show.
Copyright law exists to protect authors' rights.
Countries' laws about drugs vary, but most are, rightly, pretty strict.
Grandmothers' memories were invited for the website.
Let's all ask for our grannies' thoughts.

Exercise 4.6

Sample sentences:

1.   My bus pass is invalid so I must renew it.
      Although she has arthritis, her grandmother is determined not to become an invalid.

2.   Every minute seemed to last an hour.
      Her brooch was minute but looked good on her small figure.

3.   The second hand on my watch has stuck.
      Will you second my nomination for school council?

4.   We often have to collect parcels from the post office.
      The Vicar said the collect for the day which, on Easter Sunday, is a beautiful prayer.

5.   The pop star had signed a new recording contract.
      If hot metal cools it will contract.

6.   *Reader's Digest* is my Grandpa's favourite publication.
     I cannot digest very fresh bread without getting tummy ache.

7.   She has decided to learn the viola because she loves its mellow tone.
     The viola is a wild pansy.

8.   James cried for a long time and his mother couldn't console him.
     Dad is very proud of his new console which includes a CD player along with DVD facility and radio.

9.   'I think I can rejoin the split in the wood', the cabinetmaker told us.
     Amelia was inclined to rejoin rudely 'give over' or 'surely not' if she didn't agree with what we were saying.

10. The official promised to process my passport application very quickly.
     On 14th July many people process though the streets of Paris to celebrate Bastille Day.

Exercise 4.7

Sample sentences:

1.   My older brother is known to freq**uent** the library at university.
2.   The **con**vict in *Great Expectations* is called Magwitch.
3.   I've always been a **reb**el because I don't like being told what to do.
4.   The president wanted to retire so he didn't con**test** the election.
5.   'Why did you ab**sent** yourselves from my lesson?' demanded the teacher.
6.   'Your **con**duct is unsatisfactory,' said Mr Jones with good reason because we'd wasted a lot of time in maths.

Exercise 4.8

1.   air filled (e.g. a tyre) – pneumatic
     extinct flying reptile – pterodactyl
     poetic prayer, often sung – psalm
     doctor who treats mental illness – psychiatrist
     serious lung disease – pneumonia
     dropping of upper eye lid – ptosis
     skin disease – psoriasis
     false – pseudo
     study of ferns – pteridology
     government by the poor – ptochocracy

Exercise 4.9

Sample answer:

Mr Slope is physically repugnant with his sweaty face and damp hands. He has large, ugly hands and feet, a red face and greasy, carrot-coloured hair. He is also unattractively vain and spends time styling his horrible hair. He is far too sure of himself and plans to show the people of Barchester how they should live. He is going to upset a lot of people.

Exercise 4.10

Sample answer:

I am willing to marry the Count's daughter but only on my own terms. I expect total obedience and require that my wife not so much as smile at another man, not even a portrait painter. If the Count's daughter becomes my wife and falls short of my expectations, I shall have her killed as I did my previous wife. I don't talk about these things or plead or offer second chances. I simply take action. Please make this clear to your employer and to his daughter.

Chapter 5

Exercise 5.1

1. North's translation of Plutarch is prose. Shakespeare has reworked it as poetry into his usual iambic pentameter and blank verse (five foot, unrhymed lines).

2. Cleopatra was sailing on the River Cydnus.

3. The vessel was rowed by a team of oarsmen using silver oars. They row to the rhythm of the music.

4. Shakespeare takes the royal colours, gold, silver and purple from Plutarch and the music which accompanies the rowing (although he cuts out the howboys, citherns and viols). He also adapts the comparison with the Roman goddess of love, Venus, and the attendance by the Cupid-like boys who are fanning Cleopatra. He amplifies these by adding the description of the fans ('divers-coloured') and an account of their effect on Cleopatra's 'delicate cheeks.' Other ideas added by Shakespeare include the image of the golden barge burning on the water and the suggestion that the water is in love with the oars and so follows them ('amorous of their strokes'). Generally, the Plutarch is more factual and the Shakespeare, unsurprisingly, more imaginative and dramatic.

5. Suggestions only: (a) The sight of Cleopatra in her barge is so remarkable that no description can do it justice. It makes any attempt to describe it in words seem like a very poor thing in comparison (b) The air movement created by the boys' fans is making Cleopatra's cheeks look pink and beautiful ('glow') so that the fans seem to be defeating their purpose of cooling her.

6. There is, of course, no correct answer to this. It's a matter of preference. Answers might comment on Shakespeare's use of poetry including his alliteration, imagery and compression of expression and/or on Plutarch's straightforward crispness. Remind students that the Shakespeare is part of a play whereas the Plutarch is a book to be read which makes a difference to style and impact.

Exercise 5.2

1. He has been watching them for nineteen years ('The nineteenth autumn').

2. It is an autumn evening at dusk.

3. He has counted fifty-nine swans.

4. 'clamorous', 'bell-beat'

5. The narrator is fascinated by the symmetry and beauty of the swans rising out of the water as a group, quite suddenly, together. He finds beauty in their noisy, rhythmic circling in the air as they gather for flight. He thinks they are 'brilliant', which here is a precise word meaning brightly shining. And they are mysterious. He also comments on their pairing habits. Swans stay together for life and the narrator watches them 'lover by lover' being gently friendly ('companionable') as they swim about in the cold water or get ready to fly away. He admires the fact that 'Their hearts have not grown old'.

6. The mood is sad and wistful. Autumn is a sad time when everything is dying away or disappearing for the winter. So the narrator's 'heart is sore'. He, like the year, is ageing. He felt more cheerful and optimistic nineteen years earlier when he 'Trod with a lighter tread'.

Exercise 5.3

1. Suggestions only: (a) fancy, stuck up, showy, unnecessarily elaborate (b) like, similar to, a reminder of (c) cheek, sauce, daring, outrageousness (d) individuality, control of one's own affairs.

2. (a) *soi-disant* (b) quasi-scientific

3. She blames the chemicals used by hairdressers. She includes perm lotions, neutralisers, colourings, mousses, gels etc. She is also critical of driers, tongs and hot rollers.

4. Hairdressers sell 'treatments' to customers. These damage the hair, but hairdressers never admit this. Instead they pretend it is the customer's fault and offer more treatments to correct the damage – which makes it still worse. So it's a vicious circle.

5. She makes a case for simple washing with very little shampoo and, perhaps, conditioner. She says hair should be left to dry rather than be fast-dried with an electric drier.

6. She has grown her hair long so that she can manage it entirely herself. She wears it in a bun.

7. Pretentious, getting above themselves, servants, witches' brew, damaged, plethora, effrontery, hypocrisy, sanctimonious, conning, abuses, less than benign. (A case could also be made for others. For its length it is a highly judgmental piece.)

The sequence of tenses

Pupils who study Latin will be familiar with the *sequence of tenses* which was, to the Romans, a very strict rule indeed. As we cover indirect speech in this chapter, and indirect questions in Chapter 6, it might be worth explaining the concept of sequence, which does of course apply in English just as much as it did in Latin.

Essentially, tenses may be categorised as either primary or historic. The sequence of tenses dictates that if the main verb is primary, any subordinate verbs dependent on it must be primary too. Similalry, if the main verb is historic, the subordinate verb must be historic.

Primary tenses	Historic tenses
Present	Imperfect (was/were)
Future	Simple past
Perfect (with 'have')	Pluperfect (with 'had')
Future perfect ('will have')	

The complication arises when the direct speech (e.g. 'I am happy') is *reported* in a different tense to the direct speech itself.

Thus:
Direct speech: 'I am happy.'
Indirect speech:

She **says** that she **is** happy	She **was saying** that she **was** happy
She **will say** that she **is** happy	She **said** that she **was** happy
She **has said** that she **is** happy	She **had said** that she **was** happy
She **will have said** that she **is** happy	

Direct speech: 'I will be happy.'
Indirect speech:

She **says** that she **will be** happy
She **will say** that she **will be** happy
She **has said** that she **will be** happy
She **will have said** that she **will be** happy

She **was saying** that she **would be** happy
She **said** that she **would be** happy
She **had said** that she **would be** happy

Direct speech: 'I have been happy'

She **says** that she **has been** happy
She **will say** that she **has been** happy
She **has said** that she **has been** happy
She **will have said** that she **has been** happy

She **was saying** that she **had been** happy
She **said** that she **had been** happy
She **had said** that she **had been** happy

Pupils will almost certainly find that they don't need to be taught this in this way, as it comes naturally, but a few may enjoy seeing the rule and comparing it with what they have learnt in Latin.

Exercise 5.4

Sample sentences:

1. Our English teacher told us that he had first seen *Antony and Cleopatra* at Chichester Festival Theatre in 1969.
2. Yeats thought the swans were mysterious and beautiful.
3. Tony Blair, Prime Minister, promised to concentrate on education when he was elected in 1997.
4. The Queen often includes her husband in the openings of her speeches.
5. The explorer asked his companion to lead.
6. My grandmother said that she had just read *Bleak House*.

Exercise 5.5

Sample sentences:

1. 'I have enjoyed playing Antony,' the actor told his friends.
2. 'I hope the new building will be finished by the beginning of next term,' said the headmaster.
3. Dr Carter declared, 'It is dangerous to whiten your teeth too often.'
4. 'Be as quiet as you can because Mum has a headache,' said Dad.
5. 'I have made plans to spend Christmas in Papua New Guinea this year,' announced Aunty Brenda.
6. Jamie explained, 'I want to go the supermarket on the way to Granny's so that I can buy her some chocolates.'

Exercise 5.6

Sample sentences:

1. I shall wear my black-as-night dress to the ball.
2. These one-size-fits-all socks are hopeless for me because my feet are so small.
3. Open-for-business teachers were already waiting when we arrived at the parents' meeting.
4. Professor Cassidy was one of those dry-as-dust speakers, unfortunately.
5. Marie gave one of her fed-up-with-school shrugs and walked away.

Exercise 5.7

Erwin – wild boar friend
Cordwainer – leather worker
Wainwright – cart maker
Cooper – barrel maker
Palmer – pilgrim home from the Holy Land
Goldsmith – jeweller
Sawyer – a cutter of wood
Chandler – candle maker
Mercer –cloth merchant
Chapman – trader
Farrier – blacksmith

Exercise 5.8

Meanings and origins.

1. yuppy – person who is a **y**oung and **u**pwardly-mobile **p**rofessional (semi acronym)
2. technophobe – person who dislikes, or has a phobia about, computers and other technology (like claustrophobe etc)
3. workaholic – person addicted to working (like alcoholic)
4. cinephile – lover of films
5. townscape – view of the city (from landscape)
6. wordsmith – writer (a fashioner of words, like gunsmith etc)
7. telethon – very long TV programme, usually for charity (from marathon etc)
8. Oxfam – charity started in 1942. **Ox**ford Fund for **Fam**ine Relief
9. Ofsted – government body which inspects schools. **Off**ice for **St**andards in **Ed**ucation
10. cyberspace – notional 'space' in which the internet works

Exercise 5.9

1. solemnity
2. columnist
3. autumnal
4. columnar
5. condemnation

Exercise 5.10

1. vigorous
2. humorous
3. glamorous
4. clamorous
5. rancorous

Chapter 6

Exercise 6.1

1. The roofs of terraced buildings more than a hundred years old are best. Semi-detached and detached houses are separated by spaces too wide for the climber to cross and are therefore no good for people who want to climb across roofs. Twentieth and twenty-first century buildings tend to have steeper sloped roofs than older ones too which makes them difficult to negotiate. And modern TV aerials and satellite dishes are a nuisance. The more decorative features on the roof the better because elaborate chimney pots, and other features, make climbing easier by providing cover for the climber, but it is not a good idea to hold onto an old chimney stack which may be unstable.

2. A good roof climber is thin and supple with good night vision. He or she has no fear of heights although sometimes claustrophobics (people who fear enclosed spaces) make good roof climbers. Anyone who climbs roofs needs to be independent-minded and to want to be different from other people. Roof climbing attracts people who see their very dangerous 'hobby' (which most people would condemn as 'mad') as a way of finding freedom. They have a similar mentality to people who experiment with drugs or undertake a very challenging sport just to test their own reactions.

3. First, anyone seen on a roof by a passer-by will be assumed to be doing a legitimate rooftop job such as repairs to guttering. Second, anyone who hears footsteps on a high roof thinks that the sound must be something else because, for most people, roof walking is simply impossible.

4. (a) roof tile with an s-shaped cross section so that the downward curve of one tile overlaps the upward curve of the adjoining tile (b) small building or structure protruding from the roof (c) roofing with two slopes on both sides and both ends.

5. Roof climbing is exhilarating. It is satisfying because it requires a lot of experience and skill to do it well. So, in a sense you can train in it and enjoy the sense that you are improving. It is liberating. Like skiers and white-water rafters, roof climbers get a 'buzz' out of the danger and the opportunity to push themselves to the limits – according to the narrator. But, of course, Vine is presenting the character as a very strange person. The reader can see that roof climbing is a totally unacceptable activity which no sane person would consider. So the deadpan, serious tone of this passage is really part of the characterisation – not a recommendation to go out and try roof climbing!

Exercise 6.2

NB 'Lotos' was the standard 19th century spelling of a word usually now spelled 'lotus'.

1. The island is strangely sleepy ('weary dream'). The sailors can see a valley with the moon still above it. There are many stems but it's all uncannily calm and the water appears hardly to be moving – even where the streams reach the coast from cliff tops so that there ought to be waterfalls ('to fall and pause did seem'). What falling water there is looks like wisps of smoke drifting downwards. The sea around the island is calm ('slumberous sheet of foam'). The sun is shining on three mountains capped with old snow. Nothing seems to be changing or moving much.

2.   They have given them each a taste of an extract of lotos, taken from the stem of the plant. This is a mood-altering drug and the sailors are immediately affected. Suddenly they no longer feel any urge to do anything (such as continue their voyage). Sounds seem remote, any activity is too much effort and all they want to do is to sit on the sand and dream pleasantly.

3.   Suggestions only: (a) without energy, spirit, interest or enthusiasm (b) foreign, strange (c) without life, dry, dead.

4.   You could pick almost any word in the poem. The long vowel sounds of strings of words like 'slow', 'veils', 'lawn', for example, which work like slow mournful notes in a piece of music. The assonance of 'snow', 'clomb', and 'woven' has a similar effect. So do rhymes such as 'awake' and 'make' or internal rhymes such as 'deep-asleep'. He uses onomatopoeic lexis to build an atmosphere of lethargy.

5.   Each verse has nine lines rhyming ABABBCBDD. The effect of this is to create a sense of wandering because nine is not an even number and the rhyme pattern is asymmetrical. Of course, it's an illusion because the poem is highly structured. There is also a feeling that the poem starts and stops uncertainly because each verse ends with a rhyming couplet. This mirrors the apathy and lack of purpose of the drugged sailors.

Exercise 6.3

1.   The Health and Safety at Work etc Act of 1974 stipulates that employers are responsible for the safety of everyone on their premises. It specifies that employers must provide a written policy explaining how they do this.

2.   The Vice-Chancellor of the University has overall responsibility for health and safety. He appoints a Chairman of the Health and Safety Management Committee to carry out the work.

3.   Particular areas in which health and safety are potential problems are radiation protection, biological safety and occupational health. (Obviously these concerns relate mainly to science, scientific research and safety in the University's laboratories.)

4.   Individuals should have read the University's Health and Safety Policy and do their best to follow the rules. If they spot anything which could be dangerous they must report it immediately. Accidents and incidents must be promptly reported too. Everyone on the premises should know where the emergency exits are and what he or she should do in the event of an emergency, such as fire.

5.   Suggestions only: (a) 'carrying out that policy' (b) 'for health surveillance purposes' (c) 'newly identified hazards'.

6.   This is a formal and serious document written to comply with the law. It has to make the policy clear to everyone involved – for her or his own safety. Because it is a legal statement it is written in very stilted language. It has absolutely no entertainment function.

The sequence of tenses operates in indirect questions just as it does in indirect speech. You may wish to refer back to the primary and historic tenses discussed in chapter 5 (pages 18-19). The same principle applies, and pupils will see tenses change in the indirect question where the main verb introducing the question is in a historic tense.

Thus:
Direct question: 'Is she happy?'
Indirect question:

She **asks** whether she **is** happy

She **will ask** whether she **is** happy

She **has asked** whether she **is** happy

She **will have asked** whether she **is** happy

She **was asking** whether she **was** happy

She **asked** whether she **was** happy

She **had asked** whether she **was** happy

Direct speech: 'Will she be happy?'
Indirect speech:

She **asks** whether she **will be** happy

She **will ask** whether she **will be** happy

She **has asked** whether she **will be** happy

She **will have asked** whether she **will be** happy

She **was asking** whether she **would be** happy

She **asked** whether she **would be** happy

She **had asked** whether she **would be** happy

Direct speech: 'Has she been happy?'

She **asks** whether she **has been** happy

She **will ask** whether she **has been** happy

She **has asked** whether she **has been** happy

She **will have asked** whether she **has been** happy

She **was asking** whether she **had been** happy

She **asked** whether she **had been** happy

She **had asked** whether she **had been** happy

Exercise 6.4

Suggestions only:

1. When approached, my brother made it clear that he was both cross and busy.
2. When the Italian Ambassador visited our school he asked why so little Italian is taught in Britain.
3. Very politely, Mum asked me to lay the table for supper.
4. Our history teacher asked us the date of the battle of Waterloo.
5. Tom queried Alexander Fleming's discovery of penicillin because he thought it might have been Marie Curie.
6. Ella went to consult the menu board because she wanted to know what was for lunch.

Exercise 6.5

Suggestions only:

1. 'Why aren't you in school uniform?' our form tutor asked us.
2. 'What time does the train leave?' enquired Peter.
3. 'Which car did you come in?' asked Granny.
4. 'Where is Newcastle?' Chloe demanded.
5. 'How many hours of prep do you have to do?' probed the school inspector.
6. 'Why didn't you vote?' the interviewer asked the member of parliament.

Exercise 6.6

Sample sentences:

1. John's **keenness** to get onto the cricket pitch was obvious.
2. Some pubs limit the number of drinks each customer may buy because **drunkenness** is so unpleasant.
3. I like the **openness** of our tutorial sessions in which we can all say anything we wish.
4. Some fashion models pursue **thinness** at the expense of their health.
5. Once the orthodontist had finished with Jessica's teeth there was a new **evenness** in her smile which she was very pleased with.
6. It is easy to mistake **outspokenness** for rudeness when a frank person often says things we'd rather not hear.

Exercise 6.7

1. brethren – brothers
2. divers (as an adjective) – various
3. groat – very small coin
4. multitudes – crowds
5. corse – dead body or corpse
6. fain – rather not (e.g. I would fain not go)
7. hie – go quickly
8. twain – two

NB 'clefts' in 'The Lotos-Eaters' is related to modern words such as cleft (palate), cloven (hoof) and (meat) cleaver.

Exercise 6.8

1. 'How dare you **flout** the rules?' exclaimed the headmistress.
    Even if you're very well off it is bad manners to **flaunt** your wealth.

2. In a civil court of law the **plaintiff** is the person who brings the case.
    Even over the phone I could hear the hungry baby's **plaintive** cries.

3. My father is a deeply committed Jew but my mother is a religious **sceptic**.
    I put TCP on my cut to stop it going **septic.**

4. Fables like *The Hare and the Tortoise* or parables like *The Good Samaritan* have a **moral** message.
    The netball team's **morale** was raised by their win.

5. It is very easy to **deprecate** tabloid newspapers which carry a lot of trivial stories about celebrities, but some of them write well about health matters.
    A new car begins to **depreciate** in value as soon as you buy it and when it's a week old it will probably be worth a thousand pounds less than you paid for it.

Exercise 6.9

Suggestions only – this list is not exhaustive:

abductee, amputee, detainee, escapee, interviewee, licensee, lessee, returnee, trustee

(Avoid words like jubilee, dungaree and fricassee which come from other languages and do not follow the same verb/noun pattern although they end in '-ee'.)

Exercise 6.10

Sample answer:

It is the responsibility of everyone in form 8B using Room 19 for English to have read this policy and to be fully aware of its contents.

Every pupil must make him or herself aware of possible risk factors in the room. These could include:

open windows

furniture left in unexpected places

trailing projector flexes

uneven floorboards

bags left on floor by pupils

damaged electrical sockets

Any pupil who identifies a risk is required to take action. If a hazard can be easily made safe (e.g. by hanging up a bag) then he or she should do it. Otherwise hazards should be reported to the teacher in charge of the lesson immediately.

Every student should know where the emergency exits are and be familiar with the evacuation drill.

Any accident or incident relating to health and safety must be reported promptly to the bursar either by a pupil or by the teacher in charge of the lesson.

Chapter 7

Exercise 7.1

1. He was a compulsive gambler. It started with playing bridge during a holiday on the Isle of Wight and led, eventually, to debts which ruined him and left his widow with nothing.

2. She became pregnant while still a student. She refused either to settle down with the baby's father or to have the child adopted.

3. Her step-grandfather had been left sterile by mumps in puberty. Their marriage predated modern reproductive technology so there was nothing they could do.

4. She went to a caravan in Shropshire.

5. She is envious of Gran's age, experience and certainty. She is feeling very unsure of herself. For Gran, the sort of worries the narrator is coping with now are a long way behind her.

6. Gran is on holiday with her friend Beatrice. They are staying on the Pacific coast (probably in, for instance, California). The narrator imagines them smoking, perhaps something other than tobacco.

Exercise 7.2

1. Two are working away from home in the navy. Two more live away at Conway. Jane and John are dead. The little girl, who is speaking to the narrator, lives in the cottage next to the churchyard with her mother. That makes seven.

2. She insists that she is one of seven children, although two of her siblings are dead. That's why Wordsworth makes her tell the narrator four times that they are seven. It's repeated in the poem's title too.

3. The most striking thing is the simple language. It is mostly monosyllabic and there are few Latin-derived words. It makes the poem timeless (very close to the language of today) and emphasises the naturalness and certainty of the little girl.

4. She has thick, curly hair, pretty eyes and country beauty. Her clothes are 'wild' or very basic and unstylish. She is eight years old.

5. It is a religious poem because, for the little girl, death has not separated her from her brother and sister. As far as she is concerned they still exist (in heaven) and are still part of the family, although she understands that they are physically dead because she describes their deaths and burials. The narrator is admiring her faith and confidence and inviting the reader to do the same.

Exercise 7.3

1. A taboo subject is something which custom or convention does not allow to be openly discussed.

2.   The writer's father was blind ('my father's blindness') so presumably his mother had to be his carer. But the implication is that his father was a difficult man. The disability wasn't talked about and Mrs Mortimer was generally regarded 'as a heroine and a saint' for 'putting up with' her husband.

3.   She was teaching at Natal in South Africa, having studied art at college, when she was sent a newspaper cutting about her father's suicide.

4.   She was an atheist. She had 'no use at all for God'.

5.   Suggestions only: (a) strong, impressive, indomitable (b) admired, worshipped, highly regarded.

6.   She was an individualist from Leamington Spa with artistic talent and a love of slightly risqué modern literature. She was a teacher. In her youth she rode horses bare back and swam in the nude. She rejected her mother's religion. In marriage she took on a difficult man who was (or became) blind. She cared for him with great devotion.

Exercise 7.4

1.   Only we read 'We are seven' that morning. (No one else read it.)
2.   We only read 'We are seven' that morning. (We didn't study it or learn it by heart.)
3.   We read only 'We are seven' that morning. (We read nothing else.)
4.   We read 'We are seven' only that morning. (We had read it very recently.)
5.   *Turbulence* is the only novel by Jan Mark that I have read. (I haven't read any other novels by Jan Mark.)
6.   *Turbulence* is the novel by Jan Mark that only I have read. (No one else has read it.)
7.   *Turbulence* is the novel by Jan Mark that I have only read. (I haven't studied, discussed or reviewed it.)

Exercise 7.5

1.   We must be sure to prepare for the exam carefully.
2.   Are you ready to pay Gran a quick visit?
3.   Mum told us that she used to like reading only books about horses.
4.   I really will try to practise the trumpet regularly.
5.   Let's get ready to have a really enjoyable time.
6.   Americans often like to use split infinitives.

Exercise 7.6

Sample sentences:

Fancy! Cauliflower cheese for supper.
Fancy cauliflower cheese for supper?

Can you wait a minute while I wash, Claire?
Can you wait a minute while I wash Claire?

This painter claims John Mortimer, the famous playwright, is outstanding.
'This painter,' claims John Mortimer, the famous playwright, 'is outstanding.'

'Let me introduce you to Sophie', Ellis.
'Let me introduce you to Sophie Ellis.'

John said my friend, Paul, is a fine cellist.
'John,' said my friend Paul 'is a fine cellist.'

Exercise 7.7

monologue – performance by a single speaker
bibliomania – obsession with books and reading
monogamy – marriage to a single partner
monochrome – black and white
trichotillomania – obsession with pulling out one's own hair
monolingual – able to speak only one language
monosyllable – a word with only one syllable
pyromania – obsession with fire

Exercise 7.8

Sample sentences:

If you grow irises you need to dig up their knotted rhizomes and divide them every four years.

Our teacher is an individualist, but that's what makes her so charismatic and why we learn such a lot with her.

Brahms wrote a beautiful rhapsody for contralto soloist, male choir and orchestra.

I tend to confuse geometric figures with four angles and sides so I have to work hard to remember that the rhombus is the one which is like a square pushed sideways.

Rufus didn't get a solo part in *Annie* but he thoroughly enjoyed singing in the chorus.

Because my neighbour has severe arthritis she cannot bend down to attend to her feet so she goes to a chiropodist.

Chemotherapy is drug treatment for cancer and it saves many lives.

The swimming pool I use now has a new filtration system so it needs less chlorine to disinfect it.

Chapter 8

Exercise 8.1

1. The animals had been fighting a battle against invaders of their farm – a skirmish known thereafter as 'The Battle of the Windmill'. It has led to the destruction of the windmill and two years' painstaking work. Some of the animals have been killed in the fighting and others are injured.

2. Squealer, like many leaders in battles, did not fight in the front line. He has saved himself by keeping out of the way. The ordinary animals have not realised that this was an act of self-interest or cowardice but they are puzzled. But Orwell lets the reader see 'past' the animals' reaction so that we know the truth.

3. Napoleon is the top leader. He uses ceremony to impress the animals. He walks at the front of the funeral procession and takes credit for the 'victory' (which was really a defeat) by creating a new honour and awarding it to himself. But he knows how to placate the ordinary animals who aren't very intelligent. He arranges for a tiny gift for each of them so that they all think they've been treated well and rewarded.

4. Boxer is a very strong worker and brave fighter. He has been injured in the battle. When he thinks about rebuilding the windmill he tries not to be disillusioned, but fears his strength might be lessening. Unlike Squealer he knows just how much physical effort it will take to re-build the windmill. He has common sense. That's why he asks about the gun and the 'victory'.

5. It is to suggest that they are all equal although clearly they are not. 'Comrade' was how Russians addressed each other after the Russian Revolution and the end of the Russian royal family in 1917.

6. The animals are governing themselves without human beings so this passage is about government. It's also about how some animals, or people, will always seize power – as Squealer and Napoleon have done – under any circumstances. The leaders are manipulating the others by getting them to fight for them and by not telling them the truth. To argue that the loss of the windmill is a victory is absurd but Squealer persuades the others. The piece (like the novel that it comes from) is a satire about the working of human government. The animals and the farm are metaphors for a race of people and a country.

Exercise 8.2

1. He imagines them sleeping well despite their poverty and uncomfortable surroundings. He wishes he could sleep too.

2. He is speaking to a personification of sleep ('O sleep, O gentle sleep'). He imagines sleep as a kind visitor who calls on people in their beds to 'seal' them into 'repose'.

3. cribs, pallets, canopies, couch, cradle.

4. Even the ship-boy, who has to rest high up on a 'high and giddy mast' out at sea where it's noisy ('deafening clamour') and rough ('rude imperious surge') is able to get to sleep. So it seems very unfair that the King in all his comfortable luxury ('appliances and means') cannot.

5.   The following are two possible answers:

     'Nature's soft nurse' uses a combination of soft 'n' and 'f' sounds with the hissing sibilance of the three uses of 's' to evoke a soothing sound. It suggests that sleep is a gentle caring companion.

     'Hushed with buzzing' is an example of assonance and consonance being used to create onomatopoeia. The vowel sound is the same in 'hushed' and 'buzzing'. Both have a sibilant consonant sound – 'sh' and 'zz'. The effect is to create the sound of the night-flies.

6.   He thinks that it is because he is King and has so many worries that he cannot get to sleep. He thinks that life is easier and more carefree for his subjects. The crown here symbolises his kingship. This line is a summary of everything he has said in this speech.

Exercise 8.3

1.   Yoweri Museveni first became President of Uganda in 1986 (20 years before 2006).

2.   Mr Museveni beat his main opponent by 23%. He got 60% and the other man got 37%.

3.   Mr Museveni's opponents argue that he was wrong to change the law so that he could become president again. If he had not done this Uganda would now have a new president.

4.   President Museveni has, during the last two decades, made Uganda safer and raised the standard of living. He is welcome to many people because he is not a ruthless dictator like Amin and Obote who preceded him.

5.   Kizza Besigye is a medical doctor. Before he and Mr Museveni quarrelled he was the latter's doctor.

6.   Dr Besigye was accused of treason and rape in 2005.

7.   The election was fair by African standards, and an improvement on previous elections in Uganda. Observers from the European Union reported that some voters were turned away from polling stations and that some ballot boxes were not properly sealed. But this can have occurred in only a few places because the general comment was that the election was 'largely free and fair.' And there was none of the violence which affected local elections five years earlier.

Exercise 8.4

1.   George Orwell wrote fewer books than Charles Dickens.
2.   Do we need more or fewer suitcases for this year's holiday?
3.   We have less luggage than usual.
4.   Kizza Besigye got fewer votes than Yoweri Museveni in the Ugandan election.
5.   This queue is for shoppers with fewer than eight items to pay for.
6.   There is less traffic on the M25 after about eight o'clock.
7.   I am trying to eat less.
8.   That means I munch fewer chocolate bars.

Exercise 8.5

1. 'Please don't lie to me,' said the headmaster.
2. Let's lie on the beach and rest for a while.
3. The old man had lain on the floor for an hour before he was found.
4. Our new carpet was very well laid.
5. 'Let us lay these lies to rest,' said the policeman, trying to get at the truth.
6. Black Colombian hens lay the best eggs.
7. 'I don't enjoy a lie-in,' lied Thomas.
8. While the twins lay on the sofa resting, Mum laid out their party clothes.

Exercise 8.6

1. I want to re-read *Henry IV part 1*.
2. Yoweri Museveni has been elected president of Uganda.
3. After the Battle of the Windmill, the animals were also very tired.
4. I shall change my library books later.
5. All formal invitations should be replied to.
6. Before exams it's a good idea to revise your work.

Exercise 8.7

1. Years passed. The seasons came and went. The short animal lives fled by. A time came when there was no one who remembered the old days before the rebellion except Clover, Benjamin, Moses the raven and a number of pigs.
   (*Animal Farm*, George Orwell)

2. The letter from Guy was still on the desk where I had left it. Wondering why I had bothered to keep it once I had read it, I tore it up and dropped the pieces in our waste bin.

   Silver, watching me, said, 'Are you going to?'

   'Am I going to what?'

   'Marry him. This guy, Guy.'

   I could hardly believe it. I stared at him. 'Of course I'm not going to marry him. I'm too young to get married.'
   (*Grasshopper*, Barbara Vine)

3. Oz is a big bloke and I am not small but it took our combined weight to shift whatever was behind the door far enough for Oz to squeeze through. I stayed outside and put my hand round it. Sandor was collapsed on the floor between the wash-hand basin at one end and the lavatory at the other, half sitting against the door, feet against the opposite wall. I couldn't see his face. He didn't seem to be breathing.

   'Is he dead?' I could only whisper it.
   (*Turbulence,* Jan Mark)

Exercise 8.8

1. Although the word 'awesome' is often misused it really does describe accurately most people's reaction to the Pyramids.
2. Midges can be very bothersome in Scotland although some people are unaffected.
3. Traffic noise is tiresome when it continues all night.
4. Wholesome food includes fruit, vegetables and home cooked dishes.
5. Mr Jones's comments about my painting were so fulsome and complimentary that I didn't really believe him.
6. Boxer and the other animals on Manor Farm found the rebuilding work irksome.

Exercise 8.9

quarrelsome – argumentative
winsome – charming, engaging, winning
venturesome – adventurous, outgoing
meddlesome – given to interfering
noisesome – loud, noisy
wearisome – tiring, tedious

Chapter 9

Exercise 9.1

1. Suggestions only: (a) unhurt, untouched, unaffected (b) impossible to get into or break up (c) change sound or pitch like a piece of music moving into another key.

2. Stephen has been shot in the neck by a bullet from a rifle and he has a piece of flying metal (shrapnel) buried in his shoulder. The blast has knocked him out and he is suffering from concussion. More superficially there are many tiny metal fragments in the skin of his dirty face.

3. It was a whole day before Byrne and Hunt and the stretcher bearers could get Stephen to a dressing station. The men were under attack and the rule was that they must first keep building up the defences and second help those with minor injuries. Men with serious injuries who needed to be carried had to wait. It didn't help either that one of the dressing stations had been destroyed by enemy action. By the time Stephen reached a dressing station it was 30 hours since his injury.

4. He is delirious first because of a fever caused by infection in his injuries and then because the seriousness of his condition is making him drift in and out of consciousness. His mind leaps from place to place and different times of his life. He thinks of the orphanage he grew up in and believes he is there. He imagines he's in a house in France with a woman called Isabelle. He half-dreams, half-thinks of his school. He feels angry and unloved. He screams for his mother (who presumably abandoned him if he was an orphanage child).

5. No, he won't die although he is almost at the point of death when they put him out in the rain to wait for transport to the temporary hospital. While he is waiting he reaches a turning point in what is really a 'near death experience'. He imagines he hears a voice urging him not to give in (to death) for the sake of the 'peace he longed for'. That would be the easy option. He has to make 'the effort of courage' and return to the messiness of life to have some more experiences. The writer wouldn't tell us all of this if the man then died.

Exercise 9.2

1. The drowning man, who doesn't get his gas helmet on quickly enough, is a victim of chemical warfare. He is being choked by poison gas which has been hurled across in capsules by the enemy. It surrounds the men in green clouds like water so, as he falls it is as if the 'guttering, choking' man is drowning.

2. There is a lot of mud. Some have lost their boots. They are exhausted ('Drunk with fatigue') and very frightened. Some are injured and they are trying to get away from poison gas. It is not surprising that they are 'Bent double' and 'Knock-kneed' or that they can only 'trudge'.

3. It was a traditional rallying cry as governments, senior officers and even family at home assured young troops that they were doing something noble by fighting for their country. In the 1914-18 war, the physical reality of front line fighting and the very high casualty rates meant that it was anything but sweet and right. Owen, who died in action in 1918, is suggesting that anyone who quotes or believes the tag hasn't been in the front line.

4.   There are many options. For example:

'Obscene as cancer' compares the devastating effects of poison gas on the human body with the ravages of cancer. The difference is that cancer develops randomly. The gas is deliberated inflicted by one group of human beings on another. It is striking, too, that the man is dead (on 'the wagon we flung him in') but the gas and its effects are still alive 'gargling from froth-corrupted lungs'.

'blood-shod' means that their feet are bleeding so badly that it is as if they are wearing shoes made of blood. The two short vowel sounds each followed by a 'd' creates a half rhyme and – onomatopoeically – a slow, dead plodding sound like their trudging. With 'limped on' which precedes 'blood-shod', the poet also uses the four syllables to suggest the rhythm of a loud human heartbeat as the men try to get away.

5.   The rhyme gives the horror of the action inevitability because you listen for the next rhyme and so it pushes the poem forward. The first fourteen lines of the poem are, effectively, a sonnet with an octave and a sestet with alternate lines rhyming until the shock of 'light' and 'drowning'. After that it's less regular and more jagged as the narrator moves on from describing events to reflect on how he is haunted by his memories of the gas-poisoned man and the immorality of sending innocent people to exist in these conditions. He links the quasi-sonnet with the rest by repeating the word 'drowning'. Most lines have three or four beats but the rhythm is jerky to evoke the danger and uncertainty of the situation. The occasional short line emphasises this effect.

Exercise 9.3

1.   He is trying to be factually very accurate. This is not fiction. He is trawling his memory for every fact he can recall. In 1916 very few people in Britain would have travelled abroad so, in one sense, it was a novelty for a young man to be in France. But, by the late 1960s, when this memoir was written many people were beginning to travel in Europe on holiday. So the writer perhaps thinks that some of these names may, by now, be familiar to the members of his family for whom he is writing.

2.   He was hurt so badly that he had to be taken away from the fighting and brought back to Britain for treatment and to recover. If he had stayed in the front line he would almost certainly have been killed as many young soldiers in the Somme Offensive were (almost 60,000 British casualties on the first day alone).

3.   He has to get help for anyone who, like William Hillyer, is injured. His job is also to catch and send back anyone who is losing his nerve and trying to slink away from the terrors of the front line: the so-called 'cowards'.

4.   Their commanding officer knew that many of the men would be killed. He therefore makes sure that the soldiers get a bit of pleasure from reading their letters and talking to their friends because they may never get another chance. It is a form of kindness in a very harsh situation.

5.   His foot was clearly very badly hurt. He needed emergency surgery and, later, many operations to remove 'pieces of diseased bone'. Immediately after the injury he was probably faint with the pain and in and out of consciousness. He may also have had an infection resulting from the wound, in which case fever would have made him delirious. And the doctors may have given him a strong pain killer, such as morphine, which would have made him sleepy and inclined to lose track of time.

Exercise 9.4

Suggestions only:

1. I have . . . walked, researched (the topic), circulated, acted (a role), wandered, composed (a song), tidied (the kitchen), worked, talked, carried (the argument), begged (him), played (football), cried, laughed, shouted, cooked (breakfast), combed (my hair), danced, closed (the door), waved.
2. He has . . . spoken, thought, sung, drunk (his water), bought (a car), sat, swum (a length), lain, struck (a bargain), driven (her car), woven (a mat), brought (his mother), written, made (a cake), gone, broken (the vase), run, read (the book), got (a horse), flown (an aircraft).

Exercise 9.5

1. It should read: Verbs **have** to agree with their subjects. The word 'has' is an example of a verb not agreeing with the subject.
2. It should read: Prepositions are not words with which sentences should end. His sentence, which ends with 'with', demonstrates the inelegance of ending with a preposition although sometimes it's unavoidable. (Winston Churchill once joked 'Up with which I will not put' to show how clumsy slavish avoidance of prepositions at the end of sentences can be.)
3. 'And' is a conjunction and he's started his sentence with it. Many writers – Dickens for example – do this all the time. Remember the beauty of the 1611 Bible too. But (I do it too!) students need to be aware of the danger and avoid doing it too often or by mistake.
4. Should read: It is wrong to split an infinitive – ever. Or better still: It is always wrong to split an infinitive. 'To split' is an infinitive and he has split it with an adverb 'ever'. Avoidance is recommended where possible, but as with point 2., it is sometimes the only way without resorting to clumsiness.
5. A cliché is an overused expression. 'Like the plague' is an example.
6. Alliteration is the repetition of initial letters for literary, visual or comic effect but it can be irritating. In the editor's sentence all the words begin with 'a'.
7. If you are being specific you would not use a vague expression like 'more or less.' You should say precisely what you mean.
8. Parenthesis means brackets. Much of what is casually put in brackets is unnecessary. There are two examples in the provided sentence. Neither adds much.
9. To be formally grammatical every sentence should have a finite verb. Without one it isn't technically a sentence. It's a fragment like: No sentence fragments. As with point 3. students should be wary of this but, like many great writers, they will want to use fragments deliberately sometimes. What fragment users are actually doing is to use an established spoken form in writing – for all sorts of reasons.
10. This is similar to point 7. Say what you mean with examples. Avoid the use of 'one' because it usually indicates that there is an unsubstantiated generalisation coming.

Exercise 9.6

Suggestions only:

1. The diversion on the M11 turned all the traffic off the motorway and meant we had to go a long way round to get to Stansted Airport.
2. My sister and I are very outgoing but my brother is more of an introvert.
3. I don't usually mind heights but when I reached the top of the London Eye everything started to turn as I succumbed to a nasty attack of vertigo.

4. Our English teacher is inclined to subvert the discussion if she thinks we're getting too far away from the point.
5. He drew a transverse section of a plant stem to show us how it looked if turned sideways.
6. The Liverpool versus Arsenal match was very exciting because it makes good football to see two such evenly matched teams turned against each other.

Exercise 9.7

1. British industry has moved away from manufacturing toward saleable services.
2. Because decorated fingernails are so fashionable my hairdresser now also works as a manicurist.
3. There were a lot of delays during the building but our school's new swimming pool is now operational.
4. Manoeuvring the car round the bend into our garage takes great skill and a lot of practice.
5. Each piece of music a composer publishes is given an opus number to distinguish it from his or her other works.
6. If you try too hard to get other people to do what you want you will be accused of being manipulative.

Chapter 10

Exercise 10.1

1.   (a) Miss Maria Ward (b) Miss Frances ('Fanny') Ward.

2.   Frances Ward married what her family regarded as a common sailor, 'a Lieutenant of Marines'. He was 'without education, without fortune or connections'. This was hard for her sisters, one of whom had married a rich baronet and the other a clergyman working for his wife's brother-in-law. It was an 'untoward choice' and an 'imprudent' marriage which her elder sisters thought she had decided on to 'disoblige her family'. Frances Ward didn't tell her sisters about it until she was already married. For a long time the two elder sisters had no contact with the younger.

3.   She married Sir Thomas's clergyman friend because it gave her a comfortable living of £1,000 a year (the equivalent of at least £100,000 in today's money). She thinks she has a right to tell her sister how she should live her life. She writes 'a long and angry' letter which upsets Mrs Price so that they don't speak for a long time. She seems to be self-opinionated and bossy.

4.   Maria Ward had a dowry of £7,000 (at least £700,000 today). Her uncle is surprised that Sir Thomas Bertram was prepared to marry her with less than £10,000. He thought she was 'at least three thousand pounds short'.

5.   It mentions money repeatedly. It comments on Maria Ward's dowry and Sir Thomas's 'large income'. It tells us about Mr and Mrs Norris's £1,000 a year and that Mr Price was 'without fortune'. It is a pragmatic, practical, even cynical, approach to the economic realities of marriage. Love is not mentioned.

6.   Suggestions only: (a) superior status (b) hesitate (c) protest (d) communication.

Exercise 10.2

1.   (a) If love changes then it is not genuine love. (b) Love is not something which becomes jokey as time passes. The image is of love as a master of, say, a Jacobean household and Time as his paid 'fool' or joke-maker attacking his master with his wit.

2.   Love is mentioned five times in 14 lines. The narrator of the sonnet (unlike Jane Austen 200 years later, perhaps) is suggesting that undying love is the basis of a good marriage.

3.   If 'true' minds – that is minds which are faithful to each other – marry then nothing can stop them having a good marriage. Real love does not change when other things change. It will triumph over death and last until 'the edge of doom', It's a very confident and attractive assertion of the power of enduring love – which is why it has long been one of the most popular of Shakespeare's 154 sonnets.

4.   I shan't be proved wrong (about the strength of lasting love). I stake all my writing and my experience as a man on it. It's effective because it's a complex message expressed very simply and directly in two lines which are almost monosyllabic. That makes sure that the couplet hammers its message home syllable by syllable. The double rhyme acts like a stopper at the end of the sonnet.

5.   Love is not weak with superficial beauty such as flushed cheeks and a pretty mouth. He is strong and cannot be hacked down by Time trying to cut him back like a crop at harvest time with his 'bending sickle'.

Exercise 10.3

1.   About £20,270. The cost rose by 13% to £22,906 in 2006.

2.   A stag party is one which the groom holds with his friends before his wedding. A similar party held by a bride and her friends is a hen party. These have become expensive because now they often involve a whole weekend spent abroad. Typically they mean a lot of heavy drinking and too much alcohol is bad for the liver.

3.   Weddingplan is an insurance company. It wants couples and parents to insure the wedding day so that if something goes wrong (such as an accident to the bride or groom so the wedding has to be cancelled) they can, at least, get back some of the money they have spent. Weddingplan is, of course, a business which wants to make money out of expensive weddings. At present only about 15% of weddings are insured.

4.   The honeymoon and the reception cost most.

5.   Most of the items on the list are not strictly necessary. It is possible to get married without special clothes and cars. The only necessity is to buy a licence and attend the registry office or church with two witnesses. There is a modest fee to the registrar whether it's a civil or church wedding or whether the clergyman is the registrar. But most people want to make their wedding into a costly theatrical event!

6.   Most services cost less away from the big cities. Car hire companies, for instance, will charge premium rates in London. This is partly because people living and working in London usually earn more so the market will bear higher prices.

7.   There are a lot of facts impartially expressed but his tone is slightly flippant ('bank balances and livers', 'a bit of change out of £16,000') which seems to suggest that David Sapsted thinks that wedding expenses have spiralled out of hand.

Exercise 10.4

Suggestions only:

1.   Once Vicky **had sung** she curtsied.
2.   Ben apologised but he **had sworn** before. (or he'd)
3.   After we **had looked** at several restaurants we chose the Chinese one. (or we'd)
4.   Before you **had arrived** we started the lesson. (or you'd)
5.   I **had played** tennis before I came to this school. (or I'd)
6.   My grandparents **had lived** in Hampshire all their lives but eventually they moved to a bungalow near us.

Exercise 10.5

11.   Contractions are words like 'aren't' and 'shouldn't' which are used in this sentence. Both reduce 'not' to 'n't' as we do in speech. More and more writers now use contractions as written styles become less formal. They are still inappropriate in, for example, legal documents or reference books. Some newspapers still use no contractions – *The Stage*, for example.

12. 'No' and the 'not' in 'don't' are both negatives. Logically they cancel each other out. The sentence should read 'Don't use double negatives' or 'Use no double negatives.' In practice many forms of spoken English use double negatives for emphasis. ('I ain't got nothing' etc)
13. Don't use signs such as & (called an ampersand) in your writing and avoid abbreviations which your reader might not be familiar with.
14. The two commas in his sentence are both incorrect.
15. He means 'Never use a big word when a short word will do.' He uses 'diminutive' and 'suffice' to show that long words should be used only when there is no alternative.
16. Exclamation marks are a lazy choice. They make writing look amateurish as this sentence shows. If you choose the right words you don't need them so they can usually be omitted. It is always incorrect to use more than one.
17. He means 'irrespective' or 'regardless.' 'Irregardless' does not exist.
18. There should be no apostrophe in the first 'its' which is possessive. The second 'it's' needs an apostrophe because it's a contraction of 'it is.' Remember that 'its' is the only possessive which does not take an apostrophe.
19. 'Groan' is a joke. It should read 'grown.' It's witty because when people hear puns – jokes depending on words which sound the same or similar – traditionally they groan because it's a childish form of humour.
20. The words 'have left' are missing.

Exercise 10.6

This is not an exhaustive list:

1. Link between two parts, e.g. in woodwork
2. Hinge between bones, e.g. knee
3. Piece of meat
4. Crack in a rock
5. Shady bar or meeting place
6. Illegal cannabis cigarette
7. Shared e.g. joint account (as an adjective)

Exercise 10.7

Here are 21 as a starting point. Pupils will think of more:

dent, died, dies, dine, done, ides, jest, joined, node, nose, note, send, sent, side, sine, site, snide, stone, tide, tine, tone

Exercise 10.8

1. compliment – a kind remark or gift (with compliments)
   complement – to complete, finish or add to (complementary colours)
2. councillor – member of a council (e.g. school council)
   counsellor – someone who gives advice or counsel
3. elusive – can't be got hold of because it eludes you or slips out of reach
   illusive – based on illusion so not really there (also illusory)
4. gorilla – large ape
   guerrilla – refers to small unofficial armies (guerrilla warfare)
5. alter – to change
   altar – holy place

Galore Park
STUDY SKILLS

GALORE PARK

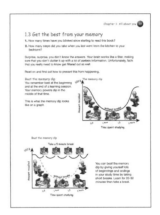

Why Study Skills?

- Perfect for any pupil aged 8–13

- Packed full of lots of practical advice about how to revise and how to be a smarter learner

- Enables pupils to identify their learning style so that they can revise using the techniques that work for them

- Includes plenty of examples of revision techniques such as mind maps and memory games which will help pupils to retain information more easily

- Workbook format enables pupils to keep a learning log which they can keep referring back to

IPG Education Publisher of the Year 2009

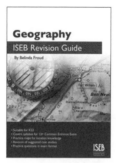

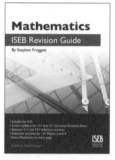